Introduction to S

History of Football Betting

The history of football betting is a fascinating phenomenon that is intertwined with the evolution of the game itself. Football betting has ancient origins, but its popularity has increased dramatically over the course of the twentieth and twenty-first centuries.

Origins and early development: Sports betting may date back centuries, but football, as a modern sport, formally took hold in the nineteenth century. The earliest forms of football betting can be traced back to the various matches between local teams in England, and as early as 1860 bets began to be collected on the results of matches.

Formalization and regulation: With the growth of the game and the creation of professional leagues, football betting has become increasingly structured. In the 60s and 70s, in Great Britain, a series of regulations were introduced, culminating in the Betting and Gaming Act of 1960, which legalized betting on various sports, including football, creating a more controlled and secure environment.

Beginning of the 21st century: Digitalisation has profoundly transformed the football betting landscape. With the advent of the internet, a large number of online bookmakers have emerged that have made the world of betting more accessible to a wide range of players. The possibility of betting in real time (live betting) has further increased interest.

Sports Betting and Culture: In many cultures,

Football betting has become an integral part of the fan experience.

Major events such as the FIFA World Cup and major European leagues attract millionaire bets and promote a thriving ecosystem of betting offers, bonuses, and promotions.

Ethical and legal considerations: Despite its popularity, football betting is not without its problems. There are concerns about match-fixing and gambling-related issues such as addiction. Many countries have tried to address these challenges with stricter regulations and social responsibility measures.

Chapter 1: Fundamentals of Football Betting

Single Bets:

These are the simplest bets. You bet on a single sporting event, such as a specific team or player to win a match. If the prediction is correct, the bet pays out according to the odds set by the bookmakers.

Multiple Bets:

Multiple (or combined) bets involve choosing multiple sporting events in a single bet. In this case, you must guess the outcome of all the events chosen for the bet to be a winner. Even though they have the potential to pay out larger sums, the risk is higher than with single bets, as a mistake in one of the predictions leads to the loss of the entire bet.

Systematic Betting:

Systematic betting is a more complex form of multiple bets. They allow you to bet on different combinations of events. For example, you can select a certain number of events and specify a minimum number of correct predictions required to win. This type of bet increases the chances of winning because it offers varying degrees of success.

Outcome Betting:

In this type of bet, the final outcome of a match or event is predicted. This can be betting on who will win, who will lose, or if there will be a draw.

Goalscorer Betting:

A bet is placed on who will score a goal during the match. It is common in football, where you can bet on a specific goalscorer or multiple goalscorers. In some cases, there are also bets on "anytime goalscorer" or "first goal scorer".

Number of Goals Betting:

These bets focus on the total number of goals scored in a match. Bets can be made on "Over/Under", where you bet on whether the number of total goals will be above or below a certain threshold set by the bookmaker (e.g., Over 2.5 goals or Under 2.5 goals).

Live Betting: Bets placed while the event is in progress, with odds changing in real time.

Asian Betting: A betting system that offers a half-point to reduce the risk of a draw.

Future Betting: Betting on events that will take place in the future, such as the winner of a tournament or an entire league.

The choice of bet type depends on personal preference, knowledge of the sport in question and your own gambling strategy. As always, it's crucial to bet responsibly.

AND ODDS

The odds represent the probability of a certain event according to a bookmaker. They express how much a bettor can earn if they win against the stake. Units can be presented in a variety of formats, including:

Decimal Odds:

Commonly used in Europe. For example, if a team has odds of 2.00, it means that for every euro wagered, you can win €2 (including the starting capital).

Fractional Odds:

Mainly used in the UK. For example, odds of 5/1 means that if you bet €1 and win, you earn €5 on top of your initial euro.

American odds:

They can be positive or negative. Odds of +200 indicate profit on a bet of $100, while odds of -150 indicate how much you need to bet to win $100.

How to Interpret Dimensions

Odds are not only an indication of how much you can win, but they also represent an estimate of how likely an event will be to succeed. Bookmakers calculate them based on several factors, such as:

Team or player statistics
Current conditions, such as injury or recent form
External factors, such as the location of the event

For example, lower odds suggest that an outcome is considered more likely. If a team has odds of 1.50, the bookmaker sees them as favorites. Conversely, odds of 5.00 indicate that the team is considered an underdog.

How Odds Work in the Context of Betting

Implied probabilities can be calculated from odds. For example:
Decimal odds: The implied probability (P) can be calculated as (P = $\frac{1}{\text{odd}}$). For example, odds of 2.00 implies a 50% probability (1/2.00 = 0.50).

- **Fractional odds:** To convert a fractional odds of 5/1 into probability, the formula is used ($P = \frac{1}{(\text{numerator} + \text{denominator})} = \frac{1}{5+1} = \frac{1}{6} \approx 16.67\%$).

These odds do not always match the true probability of an event, because bookmakers include a margin to guarantee profit, known as "vig" or "juice".

Understanding the odds and odds is crucial for anyone looking to make informed bets. It is important to analyze not only the odds and odds offered, but also to consider the external aspects that could affect the results.

Chapter 2: Team and Player Analysis

Training and Form Status:

Formation: Refers to the composition of the team in a given match. Coaches choose players based on various considerations, including injuries, fatigue, tactics, and even opponents. The formation can include various tactical schemes, such as 4-3-3, 3-5-2, etc., and greatly affects the course of the match.

Form Status: Indicates the current performance level of a team or individual player. It is often evaluated through the last games played, the results obtained, individual and collective performances. A team in good shape often breaks expectations, while a team going through a difficult period can struggle to achieve positive results.

Statistics and Trends

Statistics are essential to evaluate the performance of teams over time. Some of the most common statistics include:

Points earned: Points earned in the last matches.

Goals scored/conceded: Balance between goals scored and conceded.

Ball Possession Percentage: Indicates how long a team has owned the ball during a match.

- **Shots on Target:** Number of shot attempts that resulted in a save or goal.

Trends emerge from the analysis of these statistics over time. For example, a team might be in a positive trend if they have performed well in their last five games, or they might have a negative trend if they have suffered a lot of defeats.

Past Performance Analysis:

Past performance analysis is based on examining previous games to identify strengths and weaknesses. This includes:

Results Against Similar Opponents: The team's ability to perform well against teams of a similar level.

Performance at crucial moments: How the team behaves in situations that matter, for example, in the last minutes or in high-pressure matches.

Injuries and suspensions: The absence of key players can affect the overall performance of the team.

Effect of Home and Away Performance:

A team's performance can vary significantly between home and away games. This is often due to various factors:

Field advantage: Teams tend to perform better in home games, thanks to the support of the fans and familiarity with the field.

External pressure: Away games can come with more psychological pressure. Teams may feel disadvantaged due to unfamiliar environments and opposing support.

Fogistical factors: Travel and fatigue can affect performance, especially in competitions with close matches.

In summary, a comprehensive assessment of a team's lineup, its form, statistics and trends, past performance, and the differences between home and away can provide valuable information for understanding the potential for success in a given sporting event.

Injuries and Disqualifications

Injuries are one of the most critical external factors in the world of sports. They can occur at any time and to any player, affecting individual and team performance. An injured athlete may be away from the field for varying periods, which can compromise the competitiveness of his team. Injury management and recovery are therefore extremely important for teams and individual athletes.

Disqualifications can result from misconduct on the field, such as serious fouls or unsportsmanlike behavior. The lack of a key player, due to a suspension, can have a significant impact on a team's game strategy and chances of winning. Suspensions can also affect team morale and internal dynamics, leading to long-term effects.

Weather Conditions and Playing Ground

Weather conditions at the time of competition can greatly affect the performance of athletes and teams. Factors such as temperature, humidity, wind, and rain can alter game strategy. For example, in high humidity or hot conditions, athletes can fatigue more quickly, while rain or snow can make the game more difficult, affecting ball control and visibility.

The type of terrain – whether it's natural grass, artificial turf, clay or concrete pavement – plays a vital role in athletes' performance. Each type of surface has its own characteristics and can favor certain athletes. For example, playing on a grass court may require different skills than on a hard court, affecting speed, movement, and strategy. Adverse ground conditions, such as muddy or uneven fields, can increase the risk of injury.

Chapter 3: Psychology of Betting

Managing emotions is a crucial element in the context of betting, as betting decisions can be heavily influenced by emotional states such as euphoria, frustration, anxiety, and fear of losing. Here are some key things to consider when it comes to managing emotions in betting:

Emotional Awareness

It is important to recognize your emotions and how they can influence your decision-making process. For example, betting after a win can lead to reckless behavior, while losses can lead to a spiral of riskier bets in an attempt to get your money back.

Planning and Strategy

- **Establishing a clear betting plan, including budgets and limits, can help keep emotions in check. Having a systematic approach can prevent impulsive decisions dictated by high emotional states.**

Relaxation Techniques

Using relaxation techniques, such as meditation or deep breathing, can help you stay calm in high-pressure situations, such as after a losing bet.

Avoid Stress Betting

Betting when you are stressed, angry or sad can lead to decisions that are antithetical to rationality. It's best to take a break and only bet when you're in a balanced state of mind.

Reflection and Self-Evaluation

After each betting session, it might be helpful to reflect on your emotions and decisions. This can help identify patterns and areas for improvement in managing emotions.

Separating Personal Identity from Performance

- It is important not to identify too much with the results of the bets. Wins and losses are part of the game and should not affect self-esteem or self-perception.

Education and Information
Knowing the odds and understanding how gambling works can provide a more solid foundation for making informed decisions, reducing the influence of emotions.

Managing emotions in the context of betting is not only about controlling one's behavior, but also about recognizing that gambling has an inherently risky component.

TILT

"Tilt" is a term commonly used in the context of gambling and betting, initially derived from the world of poker. It indicates a state of frustration, confusion, or loss of emotional control that can negatively affect a player's decisions. Here are some important aspects regarding Tilt and how to avoid it:

Causes of Tilt

Consecutive Losses:
When a player suffers a losing streak, they may enter a state of Tilt, trying to recover the money lost with impulsive bets.

Intense Emotions:
Frustration, anger, or anxiety can cause a player to make unwise decisions.

Social Pressure:
The influence of other players or bettors can increase anxiety and lead to hasty decisions.

Unrealistic expectations:
Hoping to always win or recover losses quickly can lead to poor choices.

How to Avoid Tilt:

Bankroll Management:
Set a budget and stick to it. Don't bet more than you can afford to lose.

Pause and Reflect:
If you are feeling overwhelmed by emotions, it is helpful to take a break and reflect on your strategy.

Emotional Self-Control:
Recognizing your emotions and managing them in a way that doesn't influence your betting decisions.

Set Clear Rules:
Define your own rules for the game, such as win or loss limits, and stick to them.

Education and Analysis:
Study betting strategies and analyze past performance to improve one's understanding of the game and one's habits.

Principles of rational wagering:

Maximizing utility: Rational bettors try to maximize their expected utility. This means that they evaluate the odds of winning and possible losses, trying to make choices that maximize their expected gain.

Information and Probability: Rational betting decisions are based on available information. Bettors analyze statistics, past performance, and other relevant data to assess the odds of success. This requires some analytical expertise and knowledge of the context.

Risk management: Rational bettors tend to diversify their bets to manage risk. Instead of staking everything on a single risky bet, they can spread their stakes across different options to reduce the volatility of their losses.

Recognition of cognitive biases: Even rational bettors can fall into systematic errors of judgment, known as cognitive biases. Recognizing and mitigating these biases is crucial to maintaining rational behavior. For example, loss aversion or overestimating the probabilities of rare events can influence decisions.

Evaluation of offers: Rational bettors compare the odds offered by bookmakers with their evaluations of the odds of an event. If they feel that the odds are higher than the real probability, they can consider that bet as an advantageous opportunity.

Practical applications:

Bettors analyze team statistics, playing conditions, player injuries, and environmental factors to make informed decisions.

Gambling: In games such as poker or blackjack, experienced bettors apply mathematical and probabilistic strategies to maximize their gains.

Chapter 4: Betting Strategies

Bankroll management is a fundamental concept in the world of betting and gambling in general. It refers to the set of strategies and practices used to manage one's staked capital effectively, minimizing losses and maximizing long-term profits. Here are some key principles of bankroll management:

Bankroll definition: The bankroll is the total amount of money a bettor is willing to devote to betting. It is important not to use money intended for essential expenses, such as rent or bills, to gamble.

Set a Budget: Before you start betting, it's crucial to set a bankroll budget. This amount should be a capital that you are willing to lose without it affecting your daily life.

Bankroll Splitting: It is useful to divide the bankroll into betting units. For example, if you decide to bet a budget of 1000 euros and use 10 euros units, you will have a total of 100 units. This helps you manage your bets better and avoid betting all at once.

Bet Percentage: Many experienced bettors recommend betting only a small percentage of your bankroll for each individual bet (usually between 1% and 5%). This approach allows you to manage risk and withstand any periods of loss.

Bankroll Adjustment: As your bankroll grows or decreases, it's important to adjust your bet sizes accordingly. For example, if your bankroll grows, you can increase your betting unit slightly, and if it decreases, you need to reduce it.

Keep Track of Bets: Recording all bets made, including the amounts, results, and motivations for each bet, is essential for analyzing performance and improving your strategies.

Discipline and Emotional Control: Being disciplined in following the bankroll management plan is crucial. It's easy to get caught up in emotions, especially after a series of wins or losses. Staying calm and following the plan is crucial to success.

Exit Strategies: Having an exit strategy in case of significant losses, such as stopping after losing a certain percentage of your bankroll, can help protect your capital.

Set a budget

Identify your finances: First of all, take an inventory of your income and expenses. This will help you understand how much money you have available for betting.

Set a limit:

Decide on a maximum amount you're willing to spend on betting, without compromising your financial situation. This amount should be considered "lost money" in case bets are unsuccessful.

- **Healthy bets:** Never bet more than you can afford to lose. Start with smaller bets and gradually increase the amount as you gain experience and confidence.

- **Using a percentage:** Many experts recommend betting only a small percentage of your total bankroll (e.g., 1-5%). This approach allows you to minimize losses in the event of a series of unfavorable outcomes.

- **Keep a betting journal:** Write down every bet you make, including details such as the amount bet, the outcome, and any reasoning behind the decision.

- **Analyze the results:** Reviewing your bets regularly will help you understand which strategies work and which don't, allowing you to refine your approach over time.

Stats-Based Betting

This approach involves analyzing data and statistics to make informed decisions. Bettors look at factors such as:

- **Historical Statistics:** Past performances of teams or athletes.
- **Advanced Statistics:** More complex data, such as the "Possession Percentage" in football or the "Player Efficiency Rating" in basketball.
- **Injuries and Physical Condition:** Impact of the absences of key players on the team's performance.
- **External Factors:** Weather conditions, home field advantage, etc.

Practical example:

Imagine that you have to bet on a football match between Team A and Team B. Analyzing the statistics, you discover that:

Team A have won 70% of their home matches in the last 2 years.

Team B has an average of 1 scored goals and 2 goals conceded in their last 5 matches.

Based on this analysis, you may decide to bet on Team A to win, as the data supports this choice.

Intuition-Based Betting

This approach is based more on sensations, emotions, and subjective perceptions. Bettors using this strategy could make decisions based on:

Direct Observations: How a team has appeared in recent games.

Personal Impressions: A "feeling" about a team or player.

Sports Culture: Knowledge of the sporting context, historical rivalries, or team dynamics.

Let's say you're a Team C sympathizer, which is about to face Team D. You've seen Team C play in the last few weeks and noticed an improvement in their play, despite the numbers not reflecting it. Based on your intuition, you decide to bet on Team C for the win, even if the statistics don't look favorable.

Here are some examples of bets:

Spread Betting

Soccer: Applying a handicap to a team to balance the odds.

Example: If Manchester City plays Norwich, you can bet on Manchester City -1 (i.e. they must win by at least 2 goals). If the final score is 3-1, the bet wins.

Basketball: Betting on a team with a handicap.

Example: If the Golden State Warriors have a handicap of -5.5 against the Miami Heat, they must win by at least 6 points to win the bet.

Bets on the total number of points (Over/Under)

Football: Betting on the total number of goals scored in a match.

Example: If the line is set at 2.5 goals, you bet "Over". If in the match between Inter and Roma the total goals are 3 (e.g. 2-1), you have won the bet.

Basketball: Betting on the total points scored by both teams.

- Example: If the line is set at 215 points and in the match between Milwaukee Bucks and Toronto Raptors the total points scored are 220, you win by betting "Over".

Multiple bets (Parlay)

Football: Combine multiple bets on different matches into a single bet.

Example:

You bet on Juventus, Barcelona and Bayern Munich to win in their respective matches. If all three win, the bet is a winner, and the return will be greater than betting on each one individually.

Basketball:

Do the same with basketball games.

Example:

You bet on the Lakers, Nets, and Nuggets winning their games. If all three win, you collect a larger payout.

Live Betting

Soccer: Betting while the match is in progress.

- **Example:** During a match between Napoli and Lazio, Lazio is leading 1-0. Halfway through the second half, bet on Napoli to win. If Napoli manages to come back and win, the bet is a winning one.

Basketball: Betting on current events.

- **Example:** If the Chicago Bulls lose by 10 points early in the last quarter, you can bet on a Bulls "Comeback" to win, based on how the game is going.

Statistical analysis

Use data and statistics to inform your bets:

- **Example: In football, analyze the recent performance of teams, such as goals scored and conceded, home and away. If a team has scored a lot of goals in recent games and is playing at home against a weak defense, it could be a good sign to bet on a draw or a high number of goals.**

Odds Analysis

Understanding betting odds and looking for value:

Example: If a team is given as a favorite but according to your analysis has a lower probability of winning than indicated by the odds, you may consider betting against it. For example, if a team has odds of 1.50 to win, but according to your evaluations they only have a 60% chance of winning, you may find value in a draw bet.

Live Betting

Betting during the course of a match:

Example: In a basketball game, if a team is playing poorly in the first quarter, but you've noticed that in the second quarter it tends to catch up, it might be smart to bet on it for the overall win when the odds are higher.

Betting on Alternative Markets

Explore bets on less popular markets:

Example: In basketball, instead of betting only on the winner of the game, you could bet on the "MVP" (Most Valuable Player) of the match. If a player is having a great season and has a good chance of shining in that particular game, you may find value in that bet.

Team and Player Analysis

Consider injuries, transfers, and motivations:

Example: If a football team has just lost its best striker to injury and meets a team in form, it could be a good time to bet against the injured team.

Environmental and Psychological Factors

Consider the context in which the event will take place:

Example: In a basketball game, if a team plays away in a particularly difficult arena and faces a team with a large fan following, they may have a harder time. This can affect your bets.

Follow the News

Be up to date with the latest sports news:

Example: Read articles about teams, follow social media accounts of sports journalists, and monitor updates on injuries or other news that could affect the outcome of a match.

Chapter 5: Betting Market Analysis
How bookmakers work

When a bookmaker offers odds on an event, it reflects the perceived probability of that event occurring. For example, if a bookmaker offers odds of 2.00 for a team to win, this implies that the bookmaker estimates that the team has a 50% chance of winning (100 divided by 2.00).

Odds and margin

The bookmaker's margin is the difference between the odds it offers and the true probability of events. Margin is usually calculated as a percentage of total bets. When you add up the inverse probabilities of all possible outcomes of an event, the total often exceeds 100%. This difference represents the bookmaker's margin.

Example:
Suppose there are three possible outcomes in a game:

Win A:
- odds of 2.00 (50% probability)

Win B:
- odds 3.00 (probability 33.33%)
- Draw: odds 4.00 (probability 25%)

Total Probability:
- **50% + 33.33% + 25% = 108.33%**

In this case, the bookmaker's margin stands at around 8.33%. This margin is what allows the bookmaker to have a profit in the long run.

Types of margins

Margins can vary depending on several factors:

- **Type of sport:** More popular sports such as football, basketball, or tennis may have lower margins, as there is more competition between bookmakers.
- **Less popular events:** For less followed events, the margin may be higher, as there is less information available to bettors.
- **Competition:** In a market with many bookmakers, competition can lead to lower margins, as bookmakers try to attract bettors by offering more advantageous odds.

Risk management

Bookmakers also need to manage the risk associated with betting. This means that they may change the odds in response to the amount of money wagered on a given outcome. If a large number of bettors are betting on an outcome, the bookmaker may lower the odds to reduce the risk of losses. Bookmakers operate on a business model based on setting odds that reflect the probabilities of events, applying a margin to ensure their profitability. Margins can vary and are influenced by several factors, including the type of sport, market competitiveness, and risk management approach.

Benefits of shopping for shares:

Best Odds

Each bookmaker may have its own odds lines, and this means that the same bets may be available at different odds. By shopping for odds, bettors can find the best offers available, thus maximizing the potential return on winning bets.

Increased Profits

Even a small difference in odds can have a significant impact on your bottom line in the long run. For example, if you bet €100 at odds of 2.00 instead of €1.80, your net gain will be higher. Understanding the differences in odds is crucial for those looking to optimize their profits.

Promotions and Offers

Many bookmakers offer special promotions and bonuses to attract new customers. By shopping for odds, bettors can not only find favorable odds but also take advantage of bonuses and promotions that can further enhance the value of their bets.

Informed Betting Strategy Comparing odds helps bettors develop a more informed strategy. Being able to see the differences in odds and understand the context behind them can lead to more rational and data-driven betting decisions.

Flexibility and Options

Having access to multiple bookmakers and their respective odds gives bettors more flexibility. They can choose where and how to place their bets based on market conditions, thus increasing their chances of success.

Live betting, or in-play betting, represents an innovative evolution in the sports betting industry, offering bettors the opportunity to place bets while a sporting event is in progress.

Live Betting Features

Dynamic Planning: Live betting odds are updated in real-time, based on event developments. This means that bettors can evaluate the performance of the teams or athletes as the race progresses, adding an extra layer of strategy in betting.

Varied Betting Options: During an event, bettors can have access to different types of bets, such as the final result, the correct score, the next goalscorer, or more detailed bets such as the number of corners or fouls.

Interaction and Immersion: Live betting offers a more immersive experience than pre-match betting, allowing bettors to follow live events and react immediately to what is happening.

Promotions and Transfers: Bookmakers often offer specific promotions for live betting, such as enhanced odds or free bets, incentivizing users to bet during events.

Real-time opportunities

Analysis and Quick Decisions: Experienced bettors can benefit from monitoring game dynamics and performance in real-time, using that information to place more informed bets.

Cash Out: Many betting platforms offer the option of "cash out", allowing bettors to withdraw a portion of their stake before an event concludes. This creates an additional risk management opportunity.

Chapter 6: Use of Technology in Betting

In the sports betting industry, analysis is crucial for making informed decisions and optimizing betting strategies. There are various software and analysis tools that help bettors, both amateur and professional, assess the odds, analyze the data, and predict the outcomes of the matches.

Statistical Analysis Software

- **R and Python:** Programming languages used for data analysis. They offer specialized libraries (such as pandas and NumPy for Python) to manipulate and analyze large data sets.
- **Excel:** Widely used for simple analysis and for creating betting templates. Users can create custom spreadsheets to track performance.

Predictive Models

- **Regression models:** Used to predict match outcomes based on historical variables, such as past performance, player stats, and game conditions.
- **Machine learning:** More advanced algorithms that can learn and improve predictions over time, such as neural networks and decision trees.

Simulation Software

- **Monte Carlo Simulation:** Simulation techniques that allow you to model different scenarios, helping to evaluate the probabilities of various outcomes.
- **Match simulation software:** Tools that can recreate a match based on statistical data, providing predictions on outcomes.

Data Analysis Tools

- **SportRadar and Betgenius:** They provide real-time data, statistics, and in-depth analysis that can be used to improve betting decisions.
- **Sports Stats:** Various websites and apps offer detailed statistics on teams and players, allowing bettors to evaluate recent performances.

Bet Management Tools

- **Tracking Software:** Tools to monitor bets made, analyze profits and losses over time, and manage bankroll.
- **Value Software:** Some tools are designed to calculate the expected value of bets, helping users identify the most advantageous opportunities.

Social Networks and Forums

- Although they are not software in the strict sense, platforms such as Reddit, Twitter and specialized forums offer spaces for discussion and information sharing, where bettors can find useful insights and strategies.

Using these tools effectively requires a good understanding of statistics and probability theory. Furthermore, while analysis can improve the chances of success, sports betting remains a risky business, and there are no guarantees of profit.

Online forums and communities in the sports betting industry are virtual spaces where enthusiasts, experts and beginners come together to discuss, share strategies, analysis and predictions. These platforms offer an interactive environment where users can exchange opinions and information, using collective experience to improve their betting skills.

Types of communities

Dedicated Forums:
Betting-specific platforms where users can create discussions about sporting events, odds, betting strategies, and more.

Social media groups:
Many bettors gather in groups on Facebook, Telegram, or Discord, where communication takes place in real-time and in a more informal way.

Prediction sites:
Some specialized sites offer predictions and analysis, often accompanied by discussion forums to allow users to comment and discuss predictions.

Advantages

- **Knowledge sharing:** Users can learn new betting strategies and techniques from the more experienced ones, thus improving their odds of winning.
- **Support and motivation:** Being part of a community can provide moral support, motivation, and a sense of belonging, especially in an activity that may feel lonely.
- **Real-time updates:** Users can receive quick updates on news related to sporting events, odds changes, and more, allowing for more informed betting decisions.

What to consider

- **Reliability of information:** Not all information shared is accurate or useful. It is important to verify sources and not blindly trust the opinions of others.
- **Ethical behavior:** Unethical behavior may emerge in some communities, such as "tipstering" selling unverified information. Users should be cautious and protect their betting capital.
- **Anonymity and Privacy:** Most online communities allow anonymous registration. However, it is crucial not to share sensitive personal information.

Examples of online communities
- **Reddit:** Subreddits such as r/sportsbook or r/gambling that offer various discussions and predictions.
- **Betting Exchanges:** Betting exchange platforms that often include forums and discussion sections.
- **Specific sites:** Portals such as Betfair, Pinnacle and others offer dedicated sections for discussion and sharing predictions.

Online forums and communities are a valuable resource for those involved in sports betting, providing opportunities to learn and exchange information. However, users must approach these resources with a critical sense and responsibility.

HERE ARE SOME STRATEGIES:

xFactor:

The "xFactor" strategy is based on analyzing the statistics and performance indicators of the teams or athletes before placing a bet. Bettors try to identify opportunities where the expected performance of a team or player may be underestimated by bookmakers, based on factors such as fitness, injuries, motivation, and other variables. The goal is to find the "X-factor" that could significantly influence the outcome of a sporting event.

In addition, this betting strategy involves placing a system by playing on the draw predictions, generally priced at least 3.00. This means that in the event of a win, the amount wagered would be tripled, thus allowing at least two more subsequent bets to be covered with each win. This detail makes it particularly profitable, especially when applied to bets on lower leagues.

In the world of football, for example, draws are extremely frequent in Serie B, while they are much rarer in Serie A. The same happens for basketball championships and tournaments and other sports

Practical Example: Imagine a football match between a high-ranking team and a team in crisis, with several injuries. An analyst discovers that the top scorer of the team in crisis is available again for the match. This factor could greatly affect your odds of winning. Betting on a higher score or a deviant outcome (e.g., a victory of the team in crisis) could be advantageous.

Error Correction:

The "error correction" strategy involves the identification and capitalization of pricing errors by bookmakers. Experienced bettors try to spot odds that do not accurately reflect the true odds of an outcome. This can happen when there is information not considered by bookmakers, such as last-minute injuries, lineup changes, or other unexpected events. Taking advantage of these discrepancies can lead to more advantageous bets.

Moreover, the error correction betting system involves a multiple bet strategy, i.e. a betting strategy in which you place several bets simultaneously. The peculiarity of this system is that you win if you guess all the results, but also if you make only one indicated error.

Usually this type of game requires manual action and the individual games on which a possible error is considered must be indicated. Consequently, if the mistake occurs on one of those games then you still win!

Therefore, assuming that we bet on all the matches of a day of a sports championship, and indicate as correction of the error a match of which we are not able to predict the result, we will obtain a victory both when that match ends as indicated on our grid, and otherwise.

Practical Example: After analyzing the statistics of two basketball teams, you notice that Team A has a 60% chance of winning based on recent performance, but the bookmaker offers odds for Team A to win that only imply a 50% probability. Betting on Team A to win represents a potential value bet, as your analysis suggests a higher probability of winning than what you bet.

Pong:

The "Pong" strategy is often associated with a betting approach based on very disciplined bankroll management and a variable betting system. This strategy is named after the famous table tennis game, as it refers to "passing" the odds, i.e. the decision to bet when you feel particularly confident in an event. Bettors who use this strategy try to increase their bets when they have more confidence in their choices while maintaining prudent money management.

It is also a hybrid system between doubling and error correction, whose name PONG is an acronym that means:

Same

Over

No Goals

The peculiarity of this system is that at least 2 of the three cases indicated almost always occur simultaneously.

As a result, this gaming system appears quite safe and in the case of odds close to or above 2.00 ensures a good profit margin.

Practical example:

Imagine that a tennis match has a favorite (Player A) and an underdog (Player B). At the start of the game, the odds are 1.50 for A and 3.00 for B. During the first set, if Player B starts to win, the odds may adjust, bringing the odds for B to 2.50 and A to 2.00. If you bet on A initially, you may now get back a portion of the bet if you place a bet on B, guaranteeing a profit regardless of the final outcome of the match.

Trot:

Strategy in "trot" refers to betting on horse racing, specifically the trotting discipline, where horses must move in a specific way (trot). Bettors can study factors such as recent horse form, past performance, track conditions, and jockey strategies to make informed predictions. Since trotting races have specific peculiarities, bettors can find profitable opportunities by thoroughly analyzing the data and statistics.

Or in football betting, to use this betting strategy, a player must bet €2, from time to time, on at least one or two events priced between 1.50 and 1.70. In case of victory, the player who uses the trotting system will bet €2 again on two other events priced between 1.5 and 1.70. On the contrary, in case of a loss he will have to increase his bet according to this progression system: 2 – 6 – 16 – 45 – 65.

Unlike the doubling strategy, in the trotting system, once the bet has been increased, it will always be necessary to bet that new amount. In the case of four losses, the trotting method involves identifying events with a higher price, between 1.50 and 1.80.

Practical Example: Analyzing a week's long races, you notice that Horse X performs well on muddy terrain and the weather forecast indicates storms for the day of the race. In addition, the X horse runs in a race where the opponents are inferior. Betting on the X horse to win is a strategy that takes advantage of both the current conditions and the previous form.

Single Bet:

The single bet is the simplest form of betting, where you bet on a single event. The payout is calculated based on the odds offered by the bookmaker.

Practical Example: Imagine you want to bet on a football team to win a match. If the odds for the "A" team to win are 2.00 and you decide to bet 10 euros, if the team wins, you will receive 20 euros (10 euros x 2.00) return.

Doubling Method:

This method involves doubling the bet after each loss. The idea is that when you win, you cover all your previous losses and make a profit.

Practical example:

You bet 10 euros and you lose.

The next day, you bet 20 euros and lose again.

The next day, you bet 40 euros. If you win, you get €80 (€40 x €2.00), covering losses of €30 and making a profit of €10.

Caution: This method can be risky, as losses can accumulate quickly and require significant capital.

Copy winning strategies:

Copying winning strategies involves observing and following successful bettors. Some bookmakers offer social betting features or platforms where users can copy bets from experienced bettors.

Practical Example: If a certain bettor has a good record of predicting tennis wins, you can analyze his monthly bets and decide to bet on the same events. If you bet €100 on a player to win at odds of 1.80 and the player wins, you will also get a return of €180.

Formula Kelly

The Kelly Formula is a betting method that helps determine the optimal bet size based on the perceived probability of success and the odds.

Formula:
- [f^* = frac{bp - q}{b}] where:
- (f^*) is the fraction of the capital to be bet.
- (b) is the quota reduced by 1 (e.g. if the quota is 2.00, then (b = 1)).
- (p) is the probability of winning (in decimal form).
- (q) is the probability of losing (1 - (p)).

Practical Example: If you believe that there is a 60% (0.6) probability that a team will win and the odds for their victory are 2.50, you can calculate:

($b = 2.50 - 1 = 1.50$)
($p = 0.6$)
($q = 0.4$)

So using the Kelly Formula: $$f^* = \frac{1.50 \times 0.6 - 0.4}{1.50} = \frac{0.9 - 0.4}{1.50} = \frac{0.5}{1.50} \approx 0.33$$

This means that you should bet around 33% of your capital on this event.

The Importance of Statistics

Sports betting is not just a matter of luck. To be successful, it is essential to base your bets on hard data. Statistics provide an objective picture of team or athlete performance, allowing you to identify patterns and trends that you may otherwise miss.

1. Past Performance Analysis
Statistics allow you to analyze the past performance of teams and athletes. You can look at results, goals scored, goals conceded, win percentages, and much more. This data helps you assess the current form of a team or player.

Comparison of Direct Statistics

Statistics allow you to compare direct performances between teams or players. For example, you can find out how a team has historically performed against a specific opponent. This can be crucial in making informed decisions.

Practical Example: If a basketball team has won six of its last ten games against its main rival, you may consider it the favorite in the next challenge.

Environmental Conditions Analysis

Statistics can help you consider the environmental conditions that affect performance. This can include the weather, the playing field, the distance traveled, and more. These factors can have a significant impact on a match.

Practical Example: In a horse race, a horse may perform better on muddy ground than on hard ground. Statistics help you identify this trend.

Analysis of Past Bets

Keep a record of your past bets and related statistics. This will help you identify your strengths and weaknesses and improve your betting strategies over time.

Practical Example: If you have bet on football matches where both teams have scored in the last five matches and have been successful, you may want to continue using this strategy.

In-depth research

Thoroughly research all relevant statistics before placing a bet. There are a number of websites and online resources that provide up-to-date statistical data for a wide range of sports.

Practical Example: Before betting on a tennis match, check the recent statistics of both players, including their performance on the type of surface on which they will be played.

Use of Advanced Statistical Indicators

In addition to basic statistics, there are more advanced statistical indicators that can give you a competitive advantage. These can include Expected Goals (xG) in football or Effective Field Goal Percentage (eFG%) in basketball.

Practical Example: The xG in football assesses the quality of a team's goalscoring opportunities, providing a more detailed view of offensive performance.

Team Statistics

When analyzing a team's past performance, it's important to consider a wide range of data. These include:

Results: The results of past games are the starting point. It looks not only at whether a team won or lost, but also at the margin of victory or loss.

Goals Scored and Goals Conceded: Knowing the average number of goals scored and conceded by a team helps you assess their offensive and defensive strength.

Win Rates: This is a key indicator for evaluating a team's consistency over time.

Home and Away Results: Some teams perform significantly differently when they play home or away. These statistics are important for betting.

Practical Example: If a football team has won their last five home games by an average of three goals per game, you may consider them favourites in their next home game.

Direct Performance Comparison

Direct statistics are another key aspect in sports betting. These allow you to understand how two teams or two players have behaved in the past when they faced each other. Here are some facts to consider:

Head-to-Head History: See past results between the teams or players involved in your bet.

Goals Scored and Conceded in Head-to-Head Comparisons: This can be an indicator of how teams have performed against each other in the past.

Patterns in Direct Comparisons: Look for patterns or trends in direct encounters that could influence your bet.

Practical Example:
If a basketball team has won six of its last ten games against its main rival, you may consider it the favorite in the next challenge

Advanced Statistical Indicators

In addition to basic statistics, there are advanced statistical indicators that can offer a competitive advantage.

Expected Goals (xG) in Football: This indicator assesses the quality of a team's goal opportunities, providing a more detailed view of offensive performance.

Effective Field Goal Percentage (eFG%) in Basketball: This indicator takes into account the added value of three-point shots in basketball, offering a better measurement of shooting efficiency.

Pythagorean Win-Loss Record in Baseball Teams: This statistical formula estimates the number of games won by a team based on points scored and conceded.

Practical Example: Using xG in football can help you better understand which teams are creating high-quality goal opportunities, even if they haven't scored many goals.

HERE'S HOW BROKERS MAKE MONEY:

Sports betting apps and brokers can make money in a variety of ways, leveraging different business models. Here are some of the main sources of income:

- **Margin on bets (overround):** Betting platforms set odds in such a way as to guarantee a margin on each event. This means that the sum of the implied odds is greater than 100%. For example, if the odds for a total event = 105%, the bookmaker collects a percentage of the total bets.

- **Betting fees:** Some betting brokers charge commissions on player winnings, which represent a percentage of the bets made or winnings.
- **Advertising and sponsorships:** Many sports betting apps partner with sports teams, events, or influencers to promote their services, thus generating advertising revenue.
- **Promotional offers and bonuses:** While initial offers may come at a cost, they can attract new customers and increase betting volume in the long run.

- **Premium services:** Some platforms offer paid services, such as in-depth analysis, statistics, and betting recommendations.
- **Responsible Gambling:** Some operators can make money from bets made by players who don't manage their budget well.
- **Online casino partnerships:** Some betting brokers operate synergistically with online casinos, expanding their offerings and potential earnings.
- **Market makers:** Some brokers operate as market makers, where they take the risk of betting and manage the odds market.

In general, most sports bettors tend to lose in the long run, mainly because bookmakers have a margin built into the odds. Statistics show that many bettors fail to exceed 50% success on enough bets to make significant profits.

According to some estimates, a successful sports bettor could achieve a return on investment of 5-10% in the long run, but it is important to note that there are also bettors who lose money. Therefore, the win average can vary widely and there is no one-size-fits-all answer.

Printed in Dunstable, United Kingdom